Life in the Laugh Lane

(The Journey)

by

Judy May

DORRANCE
PUBLISHING CO
EST. 1920
PITTSBURGH, PENNSYLVANIA 15238

Dorrance Publishing Co
585 Alpha Drive
Suite 103
Pittsburgh, PA 15238
Visit our website at www.dorrancebookstore.com

ISBN: 978-1-4809-5003-0
eISBN: 978-1-4809-4980-5

This book is dedicated to my dear husband,
Ronald Sr.,
without whose unending patience
and technological knowledge,
this work could have not been completed.

Introduction

Laughter is underrated. A simple fact. Laughter is actually a necessary part of life. Yes, you can argue that point with me—after all, I'm not a doctor—but can you argue that point with God?

He's the one who said it does a body good.

Each individual seems to have his or her own threshold of humor, just as we have a threshold of pain.

There is inane humor, dry humor, no humor, and other types in between. I pity the fool with no humor. This is the one who just doesn't get it, no matter how you try.

Once, there was a young, handsome man whom I'd met many years ago—true story. His countenance was grim, serious, and sad. A group of us (family) were all sitting in a room talking and laughing, he was there, but not even a smile appeared on his lips. It was like we were all speaking a foreign language that he didn't understand. For a brief period of time, I found myself alone with him in the room. Curiosity overtook good manners, and I asked him straight out, "Do you ever smile?"

He replied, "No."

"Well, do you like to laugh at all?" I asked.

The reply again was a simple "No."

Now, I'm not an authority on anything—anyone who knows me will agree with that—but obviously, this is not good. Unwittingly, I blurted out a prediction. "You have to learn to laugh sometimes, or smile, or you won't live very long."

A few weeks later, he hung himself in his bathroom. Now, possibly, this unfortunate man had a miserable life; I didn't know anything about him, except that he couldn't, or wouldn't, smile or laugh.

Drama will always find us; almost every day it's in our faces. Divorce, death, bad medical reports, abandonment, fights, and heartbreak. We cannot escape the trials of life as long as we're alive. There's high drama and low drama, but there will be drama!

Humor is different. It oftentimes must be sought, because, you see, drama happens, humor doesn't "happen." Thus the old saying, try to "see" the humor in a bad situation. For years, people have sought drama, and that to me makes no sense. There's plenty to go around, yet they can't seem to get their fill. More and more dramatic programming and movies rear their realistic little heads every day. Give me a good clean comedy or comedian and I'll be happy to laugh my way to heaven. Yes, it's true, funny things do "happen," but unless you actually "see" the humor in those things, then they're not funny. Sort of like the tree that falls in the forest and no one is there to hear it fall.

Perhaps this introduction makes me a master of the obvious. Please, just humor me.

Grandma Smiles

Grandma was a five-foot two-inch, 110-pound, no nonsense spit fire! Twenty-two grandchildren! There was no molly coddling for most of us, with the exception of a chosen few. If you dared to cry around Grandma, you were called a "sissy," whether you were a girl or a boy. One exception was sickness. That always brought out the soft side of Grandma, and she was always willing to help make it all better.

Sometimes Grandma would smile, and rarely would you hear her laugh. There was no playful side that I ever saw, although she did like games, and on occasion, something funny would be uttered by her. When angry with Grandpa, she would speak Pennsylvania Dutch. We would beg to know what she'd said, and finally, she would tell us something like this: "I said, 'I am going to jump down your throat, and gobble your guts out.'"

This was intended to be funny, but we all said, "Ewww." Or, she would tell us to sit on our fists and lean on our thumbs if there was a chair shortage. One time I was wearing bangle bracelets and jeans that swished when I walked; she said, "My God girl, you sound like a one-man band." To her, that was funny; to me, not cool. Only now do I see the humor in that remark.

Maybe you should know that Grandma's first husband died before he was forty. He came home one evening, laid on the sofa, and never got up again. Heartbreak and devastation, not just because of her husband's demise, but because he left her with six children between the ages of thirteen and I want to say five; I am not sure of the youngest age. Having no experience other than running a household, Grandma had to learn how to feed seven people with no income. But she was not a stupid woman, and far from foolish, so she used the resources available to her.

Grandma could sew, and she was quite creative. First, she had to take her oldest child out of the sixth grade to help her in the quest for survival. Together, they created lovely little paper flowers and such, because after all, there was no money to buy things, so they used whatever was available. The other children were sent door to door to try to sell the handmade products. If there was an opportunity to clean someone's home or office, oftentimes auntie would be handed that job as Grandma tended to the children and made whatever she could for profit. They couldn't keep the rent paid, and so Grandma took her brood and went to housekeeping in a chicken coop that belonged to her in-laws. Bear in mind, this was back in 1920s.

Now struggling to keep her little brood alive and together, Grandma soon found the children and herself going to bed hungry. There was very little help offered at that time due to the fact at that time there was no help "out there." There was, however, a neighbor who yelled on the street to Grandma and told her that she wasn't able to take proper care of the children, therefore, she (the neighbor) would be contacting the authorities to have them placed in good homes. Grandma went after her, fists flying; she said that no s.o.b. was taking her children from her. Just then, another neighbor stepped out of his house and he said, "No one is taking this woman's children from her; we're getting married, and we'll raise the children together." That's exactly what happened. They stayed together until death.

- 2 -

Mom Giggles

Mom was the third of those six children—a healthy, not quite happy woman of short stature, such as ran in the family. Mom giggled when amused, which wasn't often. She did enjoy television comedy though, and, for some reason, she would stifle a laugh when something really funny was said on one of her programs; it was like she fought the impulse to enjoy herself.

However, I got her good one time, and she had to laugh. Being the youngest of three girls, I learned a lot from my sisters, and found them to be quite interesting. My oldest sister was dating when I was eight; she was sixteen. One night we were watching television and I heard a noise on the back porch, so I went into the dining room to look out the window. Of course it was sis and her date saying goodnight. Mom knew this, and didn't want me to spy, so she called me to come watch television with her. Being fascinated with what was transpiring on the porch, I told Mom that there was a much better program going on outside. She actually laughed about as loud as I'd ever heard her laugh in my eight years. Then she got up and tapped on the dining room window.

Shopping trips for Mom were usually joyless, because I was with her and always pestered for things. On one particular shopping trip, there was an end cap piled high with boxes of sanitary napkins. I began my usual begging; there was an "on sale" sign, so maybe I had a chance, but first, I needed to know what was in the boxes. This is how I know Mom had a sense of humor: she told me that the boxes were surprise packages for teenagers. Truer words were never spoken. Mom would sometimes try to teach me some of life's lessons, like to take the bad with the good, to roll with the punches, and to never go where you're not wanted. Never go where you're not wanted seemed to come up quite frequently; maybe she was hoping I would run away from home.

Having three daughters means lots of drama, only this mama wasn't having any drama. She was always going to "lambaste" us (whatever that meant). It must have meant "go to your room," because that's where the drama was sent.

Laundry was done in the basement with an old wringer-type washer. Mom had a "pot stick" that she used to push the clothes down into the water. It was just a wooden spoon, but that wooden spoon terrified me. On rare occasions that pot stick would take a swipe at my behind if need be, and it smarted. One time, I peed my pants, and Mom was in the basement doing laundry with the pot sick dangerously nearby, but I knew I had to tell her what happened. After I confessed, Mom took off my pants. I started crying because I was gonna get it on the bare bottom, but Mom giggled, and put my underwear in the washer.

Here's the thing about Mom. She really had a difficult time dealing with real life drama, because it had hit her head on at a young age. Losing her father as a child was tough enough. But Mom and Dad had five children; the only boy died of pneumonia when he was one year old, the next child was a girl, and she died from a convulsion when she was fourteen months old. I cannot imagine the pain, and I never want to know. These were their first two children.

Remarkably, Mom never turned to alcohol or drugs. I think it was because of the strong support of her sisters and her mother. In fact,

Mom was the best example I've ever seen of "all things in moderation." And I am sure it was a very long time before she could even giggle. Somewhere it's written that losing a loved one doesn't mean we'll never be happy again; it simply means that we'll never be the same again. Perhaps if all five children had survived, Mom wouldn't have stifled her laughter.

- 3 -

Grandpa is Amused

Grandpa was usually cheerful and kind, but he never went out of his way to be funny. With twenty-two grandchildren to amuse him, he would often set us up to entertain him.

Grandpa owned an old pick-up truck, and sometimes, if we were lucky, he would crowd some of us younger ones in the back of the truck on a hot summer day and take us to a nearby creek so we could wade around and cool down. One very humid day he loaded some watermelons along with his grand brood. We put the melon in the creek to cool, and then we splashed and laughed, and Grandpa watched and laughed. Later, after our treat had cooled, Grandpa had us smash the melon and then grab hunks of the sweet cool fruit and eat our fill.

On rare occasions, it was just Grandpa and me in the truck, on one of these occasions, we saw a snake on the roadside. Grandpa knew his grandchildren and our various characteristics. He asked me what I would do if a snake bit me, I said I would bite it back. Not one bit surprised at my answer, he shook with laughter. That old man knew what I was going to say.

When I first learned that Grandpa wasn't blood to me, I was ten years old, and I didn't believe it, so Mom confirmed that it was true.

Then it dawned on me that his grown children always called him by name; never did they say "Dad." To the grandchildren, he was and always would be "Grandpa."

Drama was a part of Grandpa's life; it went by the name of "Grandma." That woman refused to believe that he loved her. No matter how he tried, he couldn't convince her that she was everything to him. He even told her that when she died, he would die. Grandma died in October 1982, and Grandpa died in November 1982. By the way, Grandpa was considerably younger than Grandma.

Why would she not believe the man? Because he only married her to rescue her and the children. She would not be convinced otherwise. No good deed goes unpunished.

- 4 -

A Sense of Homer

Hilarious! My dad! Homer was silly, funny, and corny, but not really witty. Just old homespun tales and jokes. Dad could make me laugh like nobody else; not a mean bone in his near six-foot, 180-pound body.

He would say the craziest things. For instance, when I was with a group of my girlfriends, he would say, "Hello, boys." Of course we giggled and protested. Then he would tell us that when we turned twelve years of age, we we'd turn in to boys, and that when boys turned twelve years old, they'd become girls. Who knew Homer was a prognosticator?

Dad would often tell me a story of how he dreamt that he was the only person alive on earth, and that he was down along the seashore selling peanuts. He said, "What do you think of that?"

I would reply, "Poor Daddy, you must have been lonely." One time after telling me this same dream, I said, "Who were you selling the peanuts to if you were the only one alive?"

He laughed, and said, "Finally!"

When Dad was having a bad day, he'd tell me that he was so low, he could walk under a snake's belly wearing a top hat. One time I asked him how a snake could wear a hat.

Sometimes, on a hot summer evening, Mom and Dad would sit around the table playing a game of hearts with another couple. It always seemed like when Dad got the kitty, he and his partner would win. Mom would get so angry, and she'd call him a bald-headed, toothless, cheating bastard. Now, you would think a fight would ensue, but no, Dad thought this was hysterical. Old Homer sat there and laughed so hard he shook all over. He loved getting Mom's goat. What a marriage!

Every day, six days a week, Dad would read the newspaper from first page to last. At times, while reading the paper, he would say something like, "I see poor old John quit drinking coffee." Such quips left me puzzled. Why is this knowledge newsworthy, I wondered.

Dad had code words for things he felt were none of my business, because I would ask him where he was going whenever he left the house. Things like, "I'm going to see a man about a dog." Disappointment was the only description I had when he returned without one. Or, "I need to get a monkey off my back." Boy did he laugh when I told him I didn't see a monkey on his back. "I'm gonna go visit Grandma." To this day, I don't know what in the world that had to do with going to the bathroom.

Dad was definitely a character. Everybody in town knew Homer. This always amazed me, and I loved when we walked together and everyone would wave or speak to him. I felt proud. "All politicians are crooks," he'd say. "Don't ever trust one." When Dad ran for local office, I sure didn't know what to think.

When I had children of my own, my dad loved to tease them just as he'd done to me. Funny thing is, he came up with a new teaser. Every Christmastime, he'd tell the grandchildren that he was going to shoot Santa Claus. Of course, the children didn't find this amusing, and neither did Mom. Mom would yell at Dad for upsetting the children, and then Dad would laugh like crazy for upsetting Mom. It became a yearly Christmas tradition.

Even though Homer was born an unwanted child and his parents sent him to work on a farm as a young boy, and even though he lost his first two babies, and even though he worked as a laborer his entire life, he never forgot how to laugh. When I went to my father's viewing, it looked very much like he had a smile on his face.

- 5 -

To Wit, Cousins

Nineteen cousins! Mostly, all of them are talented, smart, industrious, and kind. All of them are witty and fun to be around. They can find humor in anything, and I do mean anything. I'm more familiar with some than others, due to age differences, but still, I'm proud to be kin to them all. Figuring that I rank at about number seventeen out of twenty-two, it's obvious that some were grown by the time I was five years of age.

We were one of those noisy families with loud shrill voices that would get on your last nerve. That hasn't changed. On rare occasions, whenever I have an opportunity to visit with any of them, there's no lack of conversation or laughter.

As creepy as this may sound, we're at our height of humor whenever we lose a loved one. Apparently, this is how we've learned to cope with tragedy, but it was certainly not taught by our parents. We knew how to put the fun in funeral. Such behavior was frowned upon by the previous generation. Understand this—when hard hit by a loss, we grieved alone, but together we celebrated that person's life.

Six of the cousins had a strong Native American heritage; these were the ones to whom I felt a bond, spending much time in their noisy, somewhat primitive home. Age was a factor, because three of them were closer to my age. Cousin Nancy and I were particularly close, and we're still best buddies to this day. Wit ran wild in that group of clan, and it still does.

Family reunions either took place in my Cousin Dolores's country home or, if we were lucky, Hershey Park. Either way, it was raucous fun and games. Now, I know that all family reunions are usually fun, but in our case, half the fun was getting there. Transporting all of us to the park, which was about a seventy-mile trip, required some thought. Not everyone had a car or truck; some of us couldn't afford the luxury. One of Dolores's husband's sidelines was to transport dogs in a pick-up truck with a cap on the back. You guessed it! That was how six of us kids got to the reunion. Sitting on wooden benches that were placed on each side, we'd slide onto each other at every twist and turn. Oh, the joy! Such laughing! Until we emerged from the truck. Phewie! Our parents marched us off to the bathrooms. Smell or no smell, the rollercoaster and Ferris wheel and funhouse awaited us, so off we went together, arm in arm, laughing, just like the fat lady on top of the funhouse. Well, maybe not quite like her.

Oftentimes whenever we were visiting family, or they were visiting us, the children were sent off to play, leaving us to our own devices. Back then, there were no devices. Except we had one app: our imaginations. That app served us well, as we did things like play shop, or play house, or do theatrics, and always silly with laughter.

Fortunately, we knew no tragedy as children, but one could say that we had a kind of rough existence. Medical and dental problems were dealt with on a home remedy basis for most of us. Toothaches, bellyaches, and fevers seldom warranted a physician, going to the emergency room was unheard of, and if you were sick, you stayed in bed until you were better. Oh, how we suffered with toothaches, but no dentist was sought. There was no money and no insurance. Our folks were hardworking people, but we had just enough to get by, and little else.

Humoring each other was what we learned to do at an early age, and it was a great comfort.

- 6 -

Jolly Good Aunts

Four aunts! Short, short, short, and shorter. However, not, fat, fat, fat, and, fatter. Just a smidge on the chubby side. All four were Mom's sisters.

Mind you, the aunts didn't visit often, and rarely together, but rest assured, with any aunt appearance, giggles and gossip followed. Once, I overheard Aunt Beatty (Beatrice) ask my mom if my developing chest was homegrown or handmade. I was eleven. After that remark, I did all I could to hide them, including wearing a cardigan over a blouse in the summer and slumping. Enter, a few weeks later, Aunt Elsie, who critiqued my posture and suggested that I learn to walk less like my dad and more like a lady. She said, "Walk straight, with shoulders back and chest out; walk proud." That suggestion got me way more attention than I ever wanted.

Aunt Beatty was fun, though. Many an overnighter I spent with her and her husband and six children. It was almost like "anything goes" for playtime. Hide and seek in the house was always a hoot! It was always said that Beatty made the best spaghetti of any family member. Tasty, not too many spices, and filling. We had spaghetti every time I stayed over. After dinner, we were taken to the penny candy shop, each of us were given a dime and a nickel, and with that money we managed to buy a few pieces of candy, a nickel-bag of potato chips, and a small pop. By the way, we all pitched in to wash and dry the dishes and put them away, so we did earn our money. Dental problems and candy? I know, I know. But hey, we were kids and it was only once a week. Our potato chips were made, owned, operated, and sold locally, and are still being manufactured locally, to this day. Aunt **Beatty** always bought herself a large fifty-cent bag that now sells for around four dollars. She would say, "Now, kids, you have your chips and I have mine, so don't gobble your chips and then expect me to share." We gobbled, then begged, and she shared.

Yodeling requires a certain amount of talent. Not everyone can yodel. Aunt Beatty could yodel, and quite well, I might add. When Aunt Beatty hoisted a few beers, that was the very best time to ask her to yodel; otherwise, it wasn't going to happen. Therefore, the children waited until she had that third beer, and then pleaded with their mom to yodel. "Yodel la de o yodel la de o yodel la deee." It was musical like an instrument, and lots of fun, when she was finished, we wanted an encore. Our attempts at imitating her were comical, and eventually, we just fell down laughing. I do hope she knew we weren't mocking. And so concludes our story of the overnighter.

Raising six children with few conveniences and barely enough to get by didn't daunt Aunt Beatty's spirit. She loved to have a good time, and she loved to laugh.

Aunt Arietta was the mother of three children. She was also the wife of a somewhat sarcastic, self-absorbed husband. Arietta never allowed that to stifle her zest for life. Laughing eyes; literally, when she laughed, her eyes laughed with her. Many times, in the summer, she would load up a few of us, (whoever was near at the time,) and off we would go to the community swimming pool. Sometimes Arietta would get in the pool with us and splash around and play. Now this was a true phenomenon for us kids, because she seemed to be the only aunt with a playful spirit; however, she was also one of the younger ones. Arietta was quite verbal. She spoke her mind, no holds barred; if it popped in her head, it came out her mouth, mostly very funny. Telling secrets to Arietta was quite chancy.

Glenda was Arietta's last child, and her only daughter. Unfortunately, Glenda passed away as a young adult. It was a long while before Arietta's eyes laughed again.

Aunt Ebbie (Evelyn) was the mother of three and the wife of a pleasant, unassuming man. Ebbie really was jolly. Also, she was a workaholic, and extremely fastidious. All was well with the world and Aunt Ebbie, as long as you didn't muss her house, her car, or her yard. And yet, she loved to tell the story of looking after one of my sisters while I was being born. Sis was five years old at the time, and she was hiding behind a chair. Ebbie asked her what she was doing. Sandra told her that she was going to the A&P. Aunt Ebbie thought that this was so cute, a five-year=old pretending to shop. Sandra came out from behind the chair and announced that she was all done. Aunt Ebbie said, "You're done shopping already?" Sandra said, "I am done peeing." Even though Aunt Ebbie's perfect world became "soiled," she couldn't help but laugh and tell this story over and over again.

Heartbreak came to Ebbie when she lost her oldest son. He was a captain in the army, stationed in Vietnam, and there he was killed. Later, she lost her only daughter to breast cancer. Faith and great inner strength helped Ebbie and her husband through these painful tragedies.

Aunt Elsie was the oldest of the aunts, and the shorter. Remember? Short, short, short, and shorter. Elsie was the mother of five children. She and her husband divorced at some point. I was too young to remember much about what happened. Perhaps I'm prejudiced, but I have a feeling it was his loss.

A true Bible thumper! Elsie took it upon herself to see to the salvation of every soul in the family. When we saw her coming, we all scattered. To be sure, you would be quizzed about your Scripture knowledge by Aunt Elsie, and, then you'd receive the benefit of her

Scripture knowledge. Serious all the way! Elsie took Christianity very seriously. Therefore, there wasn't a lot of fun or joking around with Elsie. Perhaps she forgot that God has a sense of humor. Responsibility was really all she knew, and I believe that, in the end, she felt responsible to make sure her entire family understood that their options were either heaven or hell. One more thing I must add about Aunt Elsie that I genuinely mean with all of my heart is that when Elsie did smile, she did light up a room; it was a complete transformation from a pretty face to a beautiful face, and it was most definitely contagious! What a beauty!

All of my aunts were hard working women who did the very best they could as wives, mothers, and employees. Four lovely ladies.

Doggone Happy Uncle

One blood uncle. Uncle Jack. Jack was the father of two children and the husband of a very devoted wife and mother. "The stump of a pipe he held tight in his teeth." Yep, he sure did. Everybody loved Uncle Jack. What's not to love? Jack was average height, and he had lots of brown wavy hair and a consistent smile on his face, along with his pipe. Perpetually happy, or he seemed so, at any time I'd seen him. A most pleasant disposition. Also, above all, a gentleman. After all, he was raised by six women, and Grandpa, who was a remarkable example of chivalry.

Uncle Jack was a plant supervisor of our local water department. It seems that stray canines were attracted to such a facility, and, Jack with his big warm heart, was attracted to stray dogs. Finding homes for these pitiful creatures wasn't an easy task, but Uncle Jack took this burden upon himself and was quite successful, using his charm and popularity to accomplish the task. He was unable to convince my mother, however, so I had a dogless childhood. Jack was a part-time car salesman, along with working his full time job. He was also a musician and singer, singing duets with his wife. Mostly they recorded gospel and patriotic music. Uncle Jack was just a happy-go-lucky type of fellow. In all honesty, I know of no serious drama in Jack's life other than the pain he may have felt for his sisters' losses. In the end, however, even though he was the youngest of Grandma's children, sadly, he was the first to pass away. That darn pipe!

- 8 -

Seriously Silly Sisters

Two sisters. Janet, the oldest, and would you believe, average height, and Sandra, another shorty. Janet was sort of moody, and, she kept to herself for the most part, whereas Sandra was dramatic and excitable. Even so, it took very little coaxing to evoke a laugh from either one.

When Janet laughed, I mean really laughed, her face would turn red, and then came the tears. Now, when Sandra laughed, she would start with a chuckle, then a full blown head-thrown-back guffaw.

Growing up in a household with these two wasn't always a fun experience, perhaps because of the age difference. Sandra liked to spy on me, and, Janet liked to pinch my cheeks. I must have really liked them though, because I distinctly remember crying when they would leave for school in the morning.

One Christmas, when I was about four, maybe five years old, Janet had bought me a gray flannel poodle skirt for Christmas. Do you remember poodle skirts? She dressed me in the skirt and then took me to her friends' homes to show off her little sister. Nothing wrong with that. However, later that school year, her class had a "bring your pet to school day." We really didn't have a pet, per se, just stray cats. Sis dressed me in that poodle skirt and took me to class with her that day. Pretty funny. She always was thrifty, and this way, she got more bang for her buck.

Then, there was the time Sandra uncharacteristically offered me a chocolate, and, with great enthusiasm, I accepted. After wolfing down that sweet morsel, she informed me that they'd made chocolate-covered grasshoppers in class that day, and I was the only person who'd eaten one. Sandra could be quite the prankster, but as you'll see later on in this chapter, she didn't receive pranking very well herself.

Sometimes, when Sandra was bored, she'd play with me in my room with the understanding that I wasn't to tell her friends; after all, who plays with their baby sister? During one of these "playtimes," Sandy wrapped herself in one of Mom's lace curtains and pretended she was getting married. At the end of the ceremony, she passionately kissed the wall. Just then, one of her friends Mom sent upstairs upon arrival walked in to the room. Sandy's friend burst out with laughter, I rolled around the bed in hysterics, and, Sandy was most definitely the blushing bride.

As adults, we managed to continue to be quite silly. Oftentimes, we'd take our kids and go to the community swimming pool in the summer. On one occasion, Sandy and I were standing in the low end of the pool supervising our children. Somehow Sandy slipped and fell in the water; she began to glub and sputter. I laughed. My daughter helped her up, and boy did I catch hell from Sandy. She was angry because I stood there and let her drown in two feet of water. I thought she was clowning; she actually thought she was drowning. All she had to do was sit upright. Jeesh! We're not *that* short! Anyway, she'd always remind me of the day I let her drown.

A white ceramic cup with a small green ceramic frog on the bottom was one of my pranks; you couldn't see the frog until the cup was half empty. Janet was visiting me one day and I gave her coffee in my prank cup. As she was sipping her coffee and chatting, she suddenly screamed, and then came the red face and the tears along with some very hardy laughter. Now, when Sandy came for her next visit, I gave her coffee in the very same cup. She sipped her coffee and screamed. I laughed, she did not; there was no chuckle followed by a guffaw. There was, however, an accusation that I was trying to give her a heart attack. To each his own cup of tea or coffee.

Uncle Jack owned a very rustic cabin in the mountains in central Pennsylvania. There was a time in the summer of, I want to say, 1977, when I asked if we might borrow the cabin for the weekend. Of course, he gave his permission. Janet and Sandy wanted in on this deal with their spouses and children also. Mind you, the cabin was small, with two bedrooms, a small sitting area, and a sink with running water. One bedroom had four bunk beds, two on each side, and the other bedroom had two beds. My husband and I wisely decided to bring a tent. Six adults and eight children. Oh yeah, and our shepherd mix, named Mac. Poor Mac had to sleep in an old junky trailer outside the cabin.

Getting everyone situated was mass confusion, but also fun. We decided that the kids would double up in the bunk beds, and two couples could fit in the two beds in the other bedroom.

Riotous is the only way to describe that weekend, unless you'd also like to include the word chaotic, and let's not forget comical. Inside the cabin, Janet's attire consisted of a thin blue nightgown, which she pranced around in like a model on the runway; she was just being silly, I think. Sandy loved to sing, and now she had a captive audience. She chose a sweet little number known as, "I Love Onions." Not only did she sing it, but she sang it over and over. You have to understand that there was absolutely no drinking of alcohol or any chemical substances involved in our weekend. My husband and I said, "Damn the black bears, where's the tent?" Sorry, children; it was every kid for himself.

Ron, my husband, is a showoff at times; this seldom turns out well. He decided the following morning that he'd go down to a very cold nearby creek (or crick, as they call it there) and bathe. Grabbing a towel, he very ceremoniously announced his intentions. Of course, we all balked at such an idea, however, Ron made it clear that he had a much better grasp of the great outdoors than the rest of us. Soon after leaving for his bath of bravado, I heard him screaming. We all ran outside and down to the creek; there he stood in all his splendor, with leeches firmly attached to his back and stomach. At first, my sisters screamed, and then they laughed at the man who knew the great outdoors.

At the age of twelve, Janet was diagnosed with epilepsy, having had a seizure in the classroom. Eventually, she became reclusive, refusing to attend school, because children can be very, very, cruel after witnessing a classmate writhing on the floor. Ignorance is a catalyst to this sort of behavior. I myself was just plain frightened of her, poor thing. If only my parents had educated me, perhaps I'd have reacted differently. Apparently, hormones can overcome reclusiveness, for she did find a mate, marry, and have three healthy boys. Sadly, she also had a stillborn, and a failed marriage. Life has never been easy for Janet; she often fought off bouts of depression. Sometimes a good joke could change her whole demeanor, so when I encounter her, I try to have one at the ready.

As an adult, Sandra and her husband Jake (whom I loved dearly) struggled with a rocky marriage and poverty; even though they were both hardworking folks, they were both lacking in skills, as we all were. They had one stillborn, and, then after that, they had two healthy girls. Therefore, hardship was no stranger to Sandy, but even so, she was almost always fun to be with, and we spent many hours together over a cup of coffee gossiping and laughing.

Sandy is no longer with us. She fought a courageous battle with lung cancer. Realizing that it's almost a cliché to say that one has fought a courageous battle with cancer, which as far as I've seen, most folks who have cancer do fight courageously. Nevertheless, not one time did she complain, not once, mind you. Even in the throes of this dreaded disease, she was still fun to be with, and we still had our coffee and gossiped and laughed when I visited. Remembering one particular phone conversation with her, I began to cry over her plight. She said, "I'm not a weak sister; neither should you be one." Upon my last visit to Pennsylvania, Sandy was in a nursing home.

We stood in the doorway to her room for a while and watched unnoticed as she chuckled at a program on television. They say "you can't keep a good woman down." Sandy was a testament to that fact. She laughed for as long as she could, as much as she could, and I'm sure she drew strength from her funny bone.

- 9 -

The Whole Fam Damnily

Old sailors never die; they just get a little dinghy. My husband, U.S.N. RMC (ss) retired chief, Ron. Even though I'm trying to keep my storyline to blood relatives, how could I possibly eliminate the father of my children? You understand. At any rate, I couldn't write this chapter by excluding him.

Bless his heart. Humor doesn't come easy to Ron—not that I am implying he's a grump, it's just that wit often eludes his senses. No, he's not a dimwit! Ron is funny by happenstance, and, of such, he laughs with us all. In fact, at our age, we're sort of a Laurel and Hardy act here at home in our daily lives, but we won't go there. If you knew Ron's mother, you'd understand his lack of humor. On our first date, he and his mother, Vera, picked me up in her car for a ride to the movies. When I got in the car, the first thing Vera said to me was that she was dying, and wanted to know if Ron had told me this tidbit. Barely knowing either one of them, and being a teenager, I had no idea how to reply. Vera wasn't a liar; she did die, forty years later. This is to give you an idea of the atmosphere in which Ron was raised.

Next, we have our daughter, Rhonda, the oldest of three children. Rhonda has a very dry sense of humor. She'll say something hysterically funny and never crack a smile. Rhonda is now a school teacher, and I have a suspicion that the kids love her because she's more animated around children. She's at the point in her career where she's teaching teachers; I have a suspicion that the teachers do not love her, because she's all business in such a setting.

Next is our oldest son, Ronald Jr. Ronnie has to be the funniest off-the-top-of-the-head guy on the planet. Even though he was diagnosed as a borderline genius, when he got on a roll, it was tears down your face laughter. Jr. was our traveler, having visited all of our United States more than one time, with the exception of Alaska and Hawaii. Making his way by working odd jobs, he used the pay-as-you-go system. Jr. for the most part educated himself, because there were no school walls that could contain him.

Next is our youngest, Mark. Mark loves to laugh more that anyone I know, next to myself. Mark has made a career from working for the same defense government contractor for twenty years, but I've been told that at work he keeps his nose to the grindstone. Mark can be a grump at times; he's a bit like his mom in that respect also, but for the most part, he's a good guy. Sorry folks, this is beginning to sound like a Christmas newsletter.

Speaking of Christmas, we had an underwear Santa when the children were young. Every Christmas, Vera would buy underwear for the kids and myself, and a shirt for Ron Sr. That was all she ever got us each year, and yet each year she wrapped them as if we didn't know what was inside. Here's the thing about it, though—at that time, I weighed approximately one hundred and five pounds, yet she always bought me size 10 underwear. Talk about passive aggressive. I always threw them out. Now, I wish I'd kept them.

Reiterating, the Chief is not very witty, but he trips over his tongue quite a bit, which can be very funny. For example, one chilly October afternoon we were at a flea market, and we were both grumpy and bickering. A vendor was selling hot, spicy cider. I didn't notice the sign. As a peace offering, he said, "How would you like a cup of spider."

I said, "How would you like a punch in the mouth?" Of course, he meant to say spicy cider. Then we had a good laugh, and to this day, on occasion, he offers me a cup of spider.

Mark sort of followed in his father's footsteps in that respect. Our youngest was always striving to be like his older siblings, naturally. At a very early age, nine months to be exact, he was walking. That was comical, because he was almost as broad as he was long at that time. By age two, he was putting sentences together quite well. However, he often got his words mixed up; a chip off the old block. For instance, when Ron Sr. was assembling a toy one time, Mark yelled out, "Read the destructions, Daddy, read the cestructions." Those words weren't too far off, on more than one level. Vividly remembering the time we were all out fishing at a local creek brings a smile to my lips. Ron Sr. had caught a good-sized fish, and Ron Jr. got excited and yelled, "Look, Daddy caught a sucker fish!" Mark was about two or three at the time, and he jumped up and down and yelled, "Daddy caught a fucker sish." Rhonda and Jr. fell to the ground in fits of laughter, but it doesn't end there. Ron Jr. made the most of Mark's faux pas by having Mark tell other people the kind of fish Daddy caught; this did not go over well with the grandmothers.

As I said before, Rhonda, our oldest child, has a dry sense of humor. She is totally the straight man. For example, we were attending a party, and at the end of the festivities, we were asked to take some leftover chicken home. I grabbed some pieces and so did Rhonda. Looking at Rhonda's, plate I said, "I'll trade you for two legs. She said, "I will see your legs and raise you two wings and a thigh." We had a golden retriever for many years, I trained him to help with the laundry, and Rhonda referred to him as my wash dog. Rhonda was a serious child, but as she grew, so did her humor. I guess in our family it was learn to laugh or you cry.

Some years ago, I want to say twenty years or more, Ron Sr. was diagnosed with a cyst on the top of his brain; we were all quite alarmed. After going to a specialist, the prognosis was benign, and long live Senior. Ron Jr. made an interesting observation, however; he said that all of the doctors were wrong, because Dad didn't have a cyst on his brain; what they were seeing was Dad's brain on a cyst. Jr. loved to tease.

The spring of 1975, I believe it was, I'd worked a part-time job in order to save money to purchase clothing and candy for the children for Easter. Chocolate rabbits and ducks and crosses, oh my! At that time we lived in a house that had a laundry room with a very high built-in cupboard that had a space between the top and the ceiling. Thinking I was being very clever, I hid their Easter treasures there, never once factoring in the warm weather conditions. Easter eve, I was excited to set up the children's Easter baskets and fill them with delicious chocolate sugary goodies. Of course, when I retrieved them from their hiding place, they were melted and misshapen. Oh, how I cried; my poor babies would be so disappointed. When the children got up Easter morning, I hid in the kitchen. I couldn't bear to see their tearful little faces. What happened? Laughter! The last thing I expected to hear. There were tears rolling down their faces, from laughter! They made comparisons that morning as to who had the funniest shaped rabbits and crosses and ducks. Oh my!

Corporal punishment was permitted in our household, preferably on the behind with open hand. Ron Jr. was a handful as a youth, and also quite big for his age, whereas I was actually smaller than he over time. He often referred to my shoes as boomerangs. Jr. was faster and stronger than I, therefore, spanking him became a huge challenge. What I would do when he ran was take off my shoes and throw them at the back of his legs to slow him down; that never worked, but he always said that when I threw my shoes, they would circle back to me like a boomerang so that I could throw them over and over again. That never happened either. He also said that I served him his milk from a shot glass. What? Never happened. Never owned one. I often wondered about the I.Q. thing, because we never had to use corporal punishment on the other two; they were smart enough to do what they were told.

Over the years, I would often help out with the grands when the parents were pursuing careers or higher learning. There was a time when I was looking after my granddaughter Rachel almost daily. During that time, I was diagnosed with type 2 diabetes. Rachel was seven. I worried about how to explain to her about this disease because I had to monitor my blood, and I knew at some point she would see this and ask questions. Then I forgot to tell her. She saw me monitoring and became very excited, like she'd just solved a mysterious puzzle. "Nana," she yelled, "I know what you have!" Boy was I relieved to hear that. At least I could now dispense with the complicated explanation. She told me that a boy in her classroom had the same thing and had to monitor his blood.

So I said, "What do I have?"

She said, "You have rabies!" I laughed so hard I was frothing at the mouth.

BOHICA! A navy term that the Chief uses quite often. Some of you may be familiar with this term. It is pronounced, bo-he-ka. Acronym for bend over here it comes again. We're not unfamiliar with a series of unfortunate events, therefore, it's an everyday word in our house. Gedunk means snack bar; scuttlebutt, means gossip. There are so many terms that it's like learning a new language. Go ahead, look up military slang and see for yourself. For instance, I'm cinc house, chief in charge of house, therefore, at home I outrank the chief, therefore, the opinions expressed by the husband in this house are not necessarily those of the management.

When Ron Sr. was active duty, he was three months out on a submarine and three months home. On his **second** tour of duty, we were stationed in Charleston South Carolina. After packing his sea bag, my husband knelt by my chair, very somber and expecting the same reaction from me. Not wanting him to leave for three months with such a countenance, I replied, (with a southern drawl) "Oh Rhett, the plantation just won't be the same without you." It worked! He was no longer somber. He left mad as hell.

During one of Ron's tours of duty, my friend Betty came to visit with me. Betty was my best friend during that time. We'd met when we were stationed in Connecticut and Betty and I worked together on the base in Groton. Anyway, Betty was born and raised in England; she had that British humor. Mac, our then part-German-shepherd mix, was part of our family. Mac would often make strange glubbing sounds while sleeping. He was lying on the floor beside Betty's chair, and soon came the odd noises, glub, glub, glub, getting louder and louder. Betty jumped up and said, "Bloody hell, I thought Ron's submarine was coming up through the floor!" You've gotta love the Brits. When Betty first came to this country, she was staying in a hotel and asked the bellhop to knock her up about half past eight. She went in to a drug store and asked for a pack of rubbers (erasers). Who says we speak the same language?

Speaking of dogs (not Betty, she's no dog), after all, they are family members—they're our fur babies. Mac was our first beloved fur baby; we adopted him at State College Pa. SPCA. He had a beautiful twin sister. We wanted them both, but we just couldn't afford two dogs. Mac was a shepherd mixed with keeshond. Actually, I don't remember his age when we got him, only that he was still a puppy. Mac traveled around the East Coast with us when my husband joined the navy. Walking Mac for the first time was very funny. My neighbor was following behind us and laughing hysterically. He said he never saw anyone walk a cat on a leash before. I couldn't convince the man that Mac was a dog. I figured that as he grew, the man would see for himself. It took a lot of time and effort to train this dog, but when I was done training him, he knew his mission in life was loyalty to the family. He became as large as a German shepherd, but with very, very thick **fur** and an extremely curly tail. Even though he was very loyal, he made it clear that he expected loyalty in return. When we would take him to the vet to get his ears cleaned, he wouldn't even so much as look at us the rest of the day. Sleeping in bed with me when my husband was gone for three months was always a joy for him. However, when Ron

Sr. came home, there was no room in bed for all three of us, so Mac found a way to communicate his feeling of being left out of bed. He strategically placed a small, obviously squeezed out, hard turd between our pillows. I kid you not! When our first granddaughter lived with us, we had a bassinette downstairs in the living room. Mac decided to keep her protected by lying under the bassinette, lest anybody besides family should approach her. We all thought this was wonderful and darling and sweet, and of course we realized that Mac had the best of intentions. Unfortunately, when Mac stood up, so did the bed. Not to worry, she was fine, but we had to place something under the bassinette after that. Poor Mac. There's no doubt that animal had a grasp of words that were spoken. One day, when we lived in Connecticut, I was taking Mac for a walk and we passed two men on the street. One of them said, "I wonder which one is the dog." After they were past, Mac whirled around and tried to bite him in the ass; now I'm not sure if he was insulted on my behalf or his.

Next came a golden retriever. Actually, he chose me. We were visiting my nephew in Pennsylvania, and this sweet little fellow sat right next to my legs the whole time we were there. After observing this attachment, my nephew offered him to me for one hundred dollars—a purebred AKC registered Goldie, oh yeah. His name was Mac. Yep, that's right. Mind you, the other Mac was still alive; old Mac was about fourteen at the time. When we brought Little Mac home, old Mac was indifferent. He was very secure in his place in the family. Little Mac was a joy and lots of fun. He was the one who helped me with the laundry. He also would grab Old Mac's leash and walk him. Oh, how I wish I had video of that adorable sight. Old Mac passed away when he was nearly sixteen years old. It left a void our lives, but he certainly earned his final rest.

Eventually, we bought a house and changed neighborhoods. Our next-door-neighbor was aged and ill. She owned a mixed goldie; his name was Max. Poor Max was left outside. Our neighbor's family would come by every day to visit her, and tend to Max also. Little Mac and Max became friends, so we allowed Max to visit our yard every day, that way the two dogs could have a play date. After our neighbor passed away, we ended up with Max. Who didn't see that one coming? Max was a sort of non-dog in that he was quiet and gentle, but not much else. There was one thing I didn't like about Max: he would kill my yard birds. This was something I didn't know until I caught him eating one, which explained why I'd been seeing some chewed up dead birds in my yard. Yeah, it was his nature, but it was making him sick also, besides the fact that I love birds. Tying up Max when outside was my solution. The neighbors complained about this. They said it was cruel, so I needed a new solution. A cow bell! A cowbell attached to his collar in order to alert the birds. Now we had a good solution. The neighbors took exception to this also, and said it looked ridiculous, and, Max felt humiliated. Hello! He's a dog. A dog with a good home and loving family. Under no circumstances was I removing that cowbell. The bell stayed.

Small dogs were never my favorite. Somehow, they just didn't seem like real dogs. A young couple we knew had acquired a baby Chihuahua as a gift; they asked me to keep it and housebreak it for them. It had no name, so I named it Chico. A cold month in February was when I met Chico. He was no bigger than a mouse, and had to be fed puppy food every three hours. Since I had two big dogs in the house, I carried Chico around in my housecoat pocket, and I guarded him twenty-four hours a day. It was too cold to place this little guy outside for even a few minutes, so I paper-trained him. When I would feed him, he walked all through his food. It didn't occur to me to spoonfeed him. That would seem silly to me because he was a dog. So I put his food in the lens cap of my binoculars. Mac and Max didn't seem to know Chico was there, or they didn't care, but I took no chances. One day, however, I needed to go grocery shopping, so I placed Chico in a very large, high box, and I shut the door to the room. Remember, he was very tiny. Upon returning, just as we stepped on to the kitchen I heard a squeaking noise and saw what at first I thought was a mouse, but realized it was Chico. He squeaked just loud enough to keep from getting stepped on, and there in the kitchen lay Mac and Max. No exaggeration when I say those two looked at each other like, what the hell is that? Immediately I scooped up Chico and immediately I knew this was an extraordinary little dog. He was smart enough to get out of the large box and somehow through a closed door and knew enough to make a noise so we didn't step on him. This wasn't only survival skill, this was his desire to find me and be with me, no matter what. Long story short, the couple gave him to me. Now, every night was a three-dog night. Chico had my heart, lock, stock, and barrel. He was my ever constant, and I his. Charisma oozed from this little guy; people would take pictures of him everywhere we went. He was a Chihuahua smooth, so his hair was short, and, he looked just like the Taco Bell dog. Chico came with a price, because he had many illnesses in that first year that nearly killed him; thank God we got him, because most other folks would have put him down. Even though we couldn't afford the money, we spent whatever was necessary to keep him alive; he proved to be worth every single penny. We took him to an amusement park one time and people just went crazy over him. I stepped into the ladies room, and when I came out I couldn't find my husband or Chico. They were surrounded by people waiting to pet him (Chico, not my husband). He was like a celebrity. When we left the park that day to catch a trolley ride to our car, people in the trolley were yelling "Look, it's Chico." No sir, I am not making that up, it's true! This same thing would happen in motels where we stayed, or just walking down the street. We had a stroller for him because of his health, and this probably enhanced his cuteness. Let's face it, we weren't Chico's owners, we were his entourage. He owned us.

Little Mac died at age ten, Max died when he was sixteen, and Chico, my baby boy, died at age fourteen. With love comes pain, I would do it all over again. So I did. Now we have two rescued Chihuahuas, in honor of Chico. It's better to have loved and lost than to have never loved at all.

- 10 -

Hodgepodge

Where, I wonder, do we acquire our sense of humor? Is it acquired? Possibly it's the "tickle down" effect, alluding to genes. Environmental? Those with whom we associate? Or those things to which we expose ourselves? How open are we to a good laugh? Personally, I think it's a conglomeration of all these things and more.

In an ideal world, for every sad tear we shed, there should be an equal amount of laughs. A balance is needed in all aspects of life. Many of us are out of balance on many levels. We can get away with being out of balance, to an extent, I believe, due to the fact that God says we're fearfully and wonderfully made. If it's true that what doesn't kill us is making us stronger, then you better be very nice to me. At heart, I'm a party girl. Problem is that I'm no longer a girl, and no one my age is throwing any parties. In all actuality, I feel like I'm in a desert with no water. Where are the laughs? Tuning in a television comedian to hear foul mouth rhetoric as grown people laugh at prepubescent nonsense, you know, the sort of stuff we giggled over when were kids, I'm hard-pressed to find a laugh there. Social media has taken away much of the gathering together for a good time. Texting jokes and sending funny things on Facebook is all well and good. I'm willing to accept the few drops of water from the canteen that comes my way, but I will not accept it as a way of life, because that is a non-life. So where does that leave me? A stranger in a strange land, and I am not alone. If enough of us strangers got together, we could create our own land, and PARTAY. Although, it would be a strange party.

Modern technology is a marvelous thing! It has saved countless lives, and has helped the wheels of commerce turn a little faster and smoother, so don't go thinking that I'm a geezer stuck in my ways. Well, you would be half right; I am a geezer. Facebook has become a national pastime; there I go again with the obvious. People are practically glued to their various phones and computers, searching with great anticipation for the next posting. I once had a Facebook page, but not for long. Using my Facebook page to look in on my granddaughter's Facebook was a big mistake. Making a comment about how rude I thought her friend's messages were nearly got me un-grandmothered, so I said, not for me. My husband has a Facebook page; it looks like a meeting of the mindless. (Oh, no she didn't.) Hey, don't go hating on me now. But really, he made a comment on his own page that someone didn't like, so they unfriended him. It was no big deal because he didn't know who the person was anyway. Nonetheless, it leaves me wondering what this person does out there in the real world when others have opinions he doesn't like. Do you suppose he's unsistered his sister? Because I know firsthand that families disagree, and, come to think of it, I haven't seen much of my family for a very long time; perhaps I've been totally undone and don't know it. Oh well their loss, for I'm a fount of wisdom, but I think there's a clog in my spout.

When the Chief worked at the Pentagon, he commuted to and from by bus. Every day when he came home, he complained about other passengers who were on their phones the entire commute. Knowing when someone is going home to do a load of laundry and then make chicken tenders for dinner is just too much boring information from a person you don't even know; I can assure you he has no interest in other people's mundane chores. Yet, they shout this stuff out over the phone like they're announcing a cure for baldness. People want privacy, or so they say, but I don't think they mean it.

Once upon a time, it was considered bad manners to talk about yourself. I'm pretty sure I broke that social rule more than once. Anyway, it was apparently not considered bad manners to talk about others; my dad used to say that if they are talking about you, they were letting someone else alone.

Personal mystique is no longer a commodity. Speculation about other people is not needed in these days, because it's all out there for all to see and hear. An older neighbor who's lived near me for twenty years now keeps to herself for the most part. Knowing little or nothing about her, I am curious, and even though we speak on occasion, you know she's from the old school, because she never talks about herself. She's unique, and so, when I hear the least little tidbit about her, I'm intrigued. Don't get me wrong; just because I don't use social media doesn't mean I'm a person of mystique. Blabber mouth is what I am. I will tell you my life's story if you care to listen. Then there are those who say that the government is doing things to infringe on our privacy. What privacy? Big Brother can listen in on my calls or spy on me in any way he wants; I don't care, because he will die of boredom within twenty-four hours.

Seldom does my cellular phone ring, few people have my number, and I own an old flip-open phone with few bells and whistles. Mostly, I keep it for emergencies; therefore, I leave it on with no fear of being interrupted during a visit to the movie or a church service. A few years ago, I went to church for Ash Wednesday. Just as I was receiving my blessing from the reverend, my cell rang loud and clear. GRRRR! That phone had not rang for weeks, I tell you. The reverend and I both ignored it. I hope it wasn't God calling me; I would hate to miss that.

- 11 -

Medical Mayhem

When it comes to medical stuff, albeit doctor visits, tests, preparation for tests, and new medications, I'm what my grandmother would refer to as a "sissy." An enormous whiner, a crybaby, a shaking-in-your-shoes deplorable basket case. Oops! Who said that?

If you can laugh your way to a colonoscopy, then I applaud you. Most people just brave through such things, completely trusting of the medical profession. This is an enigma to me. Absolutely astounding! But then, let's face it, my reaction isn't normal, and I can't change that fact—I tried.

An example of this silly behavior was when I was diagnosed with lung cancer, found in its earliest stages, requiring surgery and no chemo. This was years ago, and yes, I was a smoker; no more, though. A few weeks before the scheduled surgery, the doctor said he needed to perform the obligatory exam. Bear in mind that I was a quivering mass of jelly at the time; I cried and then yelled, "Oh, my God! Do you think I have cancer of the obligatory also?" Oh yeah, the doctor laughed. I, on the other hand, did not. It was too embarrassing.

There was a time when I was on the treadmill at my cardiologist's, and when the test was over, he looked at his assistant and said, "We need to call an ambulance."

Looking around the room, and seeing only the three of us, I said, "For who?"

He replied, "For you, of course."

"No way," I said, "I feel fine!" So, I refused. Fortunately, it turned out to be a shadow cast by my breast. Please don't think I'm advocating disobeying your doctor, because, what if it had been something serious?

Another time at a different heart doctor, she told me that because I had high blood pressure, diabetes, and was over-weight and older, I was at high risk for a heart attack. Painting such a bleak picture really scared the hell out of me, so I asked what immediate things I could do to help myself. "Do you have stairs at home?" she asked.

I replied, "Yes." Get ready for this, because I'm telling the truth.

This doctor said, and I quote, "Go home and run up and down your stairs as many times as you can." No, she was not being sarcastic or funny. Looking for the door, I immediately helped myself out of the room.

A barium enema is always a pleasant way to spend an afternoon. NOT! Putting off a colonoscopy for years, I finally got up the nerve to go through with it, only it couldn't be completed. Due to no fault of my own, because I know what you're thinking. Therefore, the next step was a barium enema. (Not in the same day.) Uncomfortable and embarrassing. Lying on a cold, hard, table with two men in the room and my Netherlands exposed, I didn't know who I felt sorrier for, them or me. Assuring me that this was not their first rodeo and that everything would be just fine, I stopped shaking. They said I would feel a little pressure and discomfort; the liars. Here's what I told them: "I'd better come out of here with a baby in my arms!" There was no baby, and the test was incomplete. C'MON! Returning from a family reunion in Pennsylvania in August 2013 turned in to a trip from hell. This was the same summer that I had the two previous procedures done, so I sometimes wonder if there was a connection, but the docs all say absolutely not, and I believe them. We'd stopped at a convenience store because I was having abdominal pains; the pain was so intense I nearly passed out. My husband called for an ambulance. After being placed on a stretcher and into the ambulance, the emergency technician asked me this: "Do you want to go to the Gettysburg hospital, or do you want to go to the Holy Spirit?" Well, hmm, I opted for medical help, and preferred the hospital. He replied, "The Holy Spirit it is, then."

Being in so much pain, all I could think was, "I'm going to heaven in an ambulance?" Even though I was born and raised in Pennsylvania, I didn't know there was a Holy Spirit Hospital. Anyway, it's a fine hospital, where I stayed for four days and was treated like a queen, for diverticulitis. They're a pet-friendly hospital, and they allowed my beautiful Chico to visit me every day, which kept me in high Holy Spirits.

When it comes down to the nitty gritty, the medical profession has been nothing but a good friend to me, rescuing me over and over again. Still, I cannot seem to reciprocate that friendship. Grumbling and distrust is what I return to this friend. But when the ordeal is over and all is well, then I smile, and, joke and love them all. Until the next time.

- 12 -

Just for Old Timers' Sake

My husband makes me sick! He's a few years older than myself, and yet he actually gets carded sometimes for a senior discount; for the love of Pete, he's in his seventies! On the other hand, I've been offered senior discounts since I was fifty. Apparently, people think I'm his mother. Being the gentleman that he is, he assures me it's because I went gray at an early age, which is true. Coloring my hair is not an option, because then I might find out it has nothing to with my hair color. Allow me to say this, though, the Chief may look better than me, but he does *not* smell better than me. Now, I know why the term "old fart" is used when referring to old men.

What is all this talk about crepey skin? Why don't they just say creepy and get it over with? And why is it directed at women? Men can be pretty damn creepy. Women go to great measures to look their best, what with Botox injections and very expensive cosmetics, and even surgery. Some say they do it for themselves; I suppose that's possible. Wearing makeup is something I do as a public service. I have to look at me and so do others. Usually, I use a small handheld mirror when applying cosmetics, because I can avoid the full frontal view that way. Being upright and mobile is my big goal in life at this point, so if my appearance offends you, look away, darling. Mom was in her nineties when she started to look sloppy; well, she never did wear makeup, except for lipstick, but she was always impeccably attired. She had lovely skin and few wrinkles; she attributed that to Dove soap and Pond's cold cream. Drooping, now that's a problem for many older women. You could nick name me Droopy and it would not hurt my feelings. I don't care, it isn't a secret, and I am not in denial. Jowls, turkey neck, fat ass, go ahead, say it, I own it all, but no one ever died of a fat ass or jowls or any such things. Have you ever seen a death certificate that read, "Cause of death, turkey neck"? Unless, of course, if they choked on one. Facial hair! Now, there you've got me! I hate facial hair! People always say for every gray hair you pluck, ten more will grow; well, I think it's the same premise for facial hair. It used to be that I could wax my upper lip and be good to go for a while; not anymore. My great-granddaughter once told me it was peach fuzz, bless her heart. Maybe on her mother it's peach fuzz. Drooping, sagging, bagging, yeah, I can deal with all that. Nevertheless, I refuse to go through life looking like a werewolf, and I realize a nice full beard would hide the jowls and the turkey neck, but I just can't seem to let myself go the distance. Quite a daily challenge, really. Please understand, I realize that many senior women look fabulous, and some age beautifully; they've most likely taken better care of themselves than I have of myself. I'm only dissing myself, not all seniors.

Help! I'm shrinking. Like I said before, I'm short in the first place. My husband calls me alligator arms. I'm convinced that as we age, we don't only shrink in height, but also our appendages; except for the nose. In my case, I seem to be squishing together like an accordion. Walking every day is my exercise; a twenty to thirty minute walk. Mostly I do this to keep the old gams moving, regardless of the weather. Unfortunately, this doesn't make me any taller. Joining a ladies' gym seemed a good idea, so I did do that. It was mostly about staying agile, which was lovely, and I made use of the gym faithfully for two and a half years. So, when a lifetime membership was offered, I jumped on it; after all, I was agile. A year later, the gym closed, and yet I was still alive. Walks are a lot cheaper anyways, but I don't believe they make you agile; if they do, then my body is keeping secrets from me.

You can be young and poor, but you can't be old and poor. Have you ever heard that before? Pondering that statement, I think I finally figured out what it means. Trips to the pharmacy. Think about it. Oh sure, even when we're young, we buy moisturizer and cosmetics. But how about all that other stuff we now need? Or, at least, I need. Support hose, denture cream, special things for incontinence, pain killers, diabetic socks, heating pads, humidifiers, not to mention all of the gizmos they come out with to make our lives more comfortable, and believe me, you will want those things that make you more comfortable. Along with Medicare comes co-pays, or you will need a supplemental insurance. Have you ever noticed that many older women carry a tote bag? Well, it ain't just knitting needles in there, honey. When our children were babies and toddlers, if we left the house, I always packed a bag for them in anticipation of their needs. Guess who I pack a bag for now. Snacks, water, juice, diapers, all the same items I once packed for the babies. Life certainly does go full circle. Upright and mobile, my mantra, upright and mobile. Seems to me that arthritis is just another name for rigor mortis; my bones are stiff, and they creak and crack sometimes when I move them. Only difference that I can see is that when you have rigor mortis, you feel no pain.

Caution! Be very careful of what you say and how you eat or dress. Also, make sure your house is reasonably clean. Try not to say I forgot, or I don't remember. Don't complain a lot about pain or discomfort. You see, there's somebody in your life who's waiting for an excuse to shove you in an old folks' home, whether you know it or not. Everybody has enemies; some of them are closer than you think, and if you don't have any enemies, you're doing something wrong.

Please forgive me if I sound whiney. Truth be told, I'm grateful to be here, and I'm better off than many others; I certainly realize that fact. Be grateful for every birthday, and never ever, be ashamed of your age. Each birthday is a gift in itself, and most definitely is something to be celebrated. At the time of this writing, I'm a proud sixty-eight years old. If any of you youngsters want to look down your nose at this old lady, just remember, your day is coming, if you're as lucky as I am today.

- 13 -

Earie Assault

Music has charm to sooth a savage breast. That's right, breast, not beast. No matter, it all has the same meaning. I believe we can all agree with that statement. Everybody loves music in one style or another: rock, opera, country, jazz, love songs, gospel, and don't forget rap, fo' shizzle. Music is a gift and mostly done by the gifted, although not always.

When I was in junior high and senior high, I somehow found myself in glee club and chorus, and in church I was in the junior choir. I don't recall signing up for any of these music activities, and yet there I was, and I'm pretty sure I wasn't handpicked, at least not if they ever heard me sing. However, I do remember thinking I could sing, and I've always loved singing. After learning the words to so many songs, to this day, I still bellow out a tune at home. This became my weapon; especially, when controlling the grandchildren. With the grandchildren I didn't need boomerangs or an open hand. All I had to do was threaten to sing. It went like this: "Pick up your toys."

Reply: "No."

"Okay then, I'm going to sing."

"No, no, please don't sing, I will pick up my toys." Voila! This weapon has also worked on Ron Sr. a few times. All I can say is that my singing voice is an inspiration for good behavior. When I sing, if I'm sitting, my dog licks my mouth to try to shut it.

Our son, Mark, loved the drums ever since he was a tyke. Possibly this is due to the fact that I placed his bassinette directly in front of our floor model stereo the day we brought him home from the hospital, and there's where it stayed until he outgrew that bed. He spent his infancy listening to Black Sabbath, The Who, The Doors, Rolling Stones, James Brown, and the Beatles. Therefore, he wasn't woken by household everyday noises.

Mark was in his school band, so he practiced the drums at home. By the time we moved to Virginia Beach into navy housing, he decided to play in the garage. After a while, he attracted a guitarist and a keyboard player from the hood. It wasn't long until we had a garage band. Bear in mind, we lived in a townhouse; you know, all the houses were connected in fours. One day a police cruiser was driving through the hood. No, not M.P.s—police. He heard the band and took it upon himself to notify a few neighbors that they didn't have to put up with the noise and they could call in a complaint. There were no calls placed. Want to know why? Because their children were in the garage and driveway listening. As long as the band played, they knew where their children were located. Don't think I didn't call in and make a complaint about that officer. I told them that perhaps it would be better if I armed these teenagers and sent them out to mug old ladies. At least we knew they were innocently making very noisy music. And yes, Mark was a member of several unknown bands for a few years.

Music is a subtle manipulator. It can cause tears or laughter, and it's everywhere! Honestly, I feel as though I'm living in a perpetual music concert. There's a time and place for everything, but these days, there's a music for every time and place. Not long ago, I was in a store shopping, and this awful caterwauling was coming from the speaker. I wanted to set my hair on fire. It amazes me as to what passes for singing, and many folks love the awful screeching. Sometimes I'll walk in a place of business perfectly happy and leave on the verge of tears because of mournful tunes and whinny singing. Most people aren't even aware of the music because it's in every single store, or office, and quite subliminal.

When watching a television program, there's always music dictating how you should feel about the scene you're watching. The same applies to movies and commercials. Even silent films weren't silent, because there was an organ being played while you watched. (No, I don't go back that far.) Sorry to say this, but it grates on my nerves. Once in a while, I'd like to watch a program and not be told how I should feel from moment to moment. Commercials are the absolute worst! Either there's blaring music or sad, sorry violins playing; this is to evoke feelings for their product, no doubt. Have you ever noticed that whenever an announcer for medicine starts spouting off about the dire side effects of that particular product, the music is always light and cheery? This is supposed to make you think, it can't really be that bad when they're playing such happy music. All I am trying to say is that too much of a good thing is too much!

- 14 -

A Walk on the Wild Side

Like I said before, I'm a party girl at heart, and, looking back, I always have been one. As a child, I distinctly remember that when other little girls were having imaginary tea parties, I had champagne parties. Very carefully, I would get four glasses from the cupboard, get a bottle of Seven Up, and pour a little "champagne" into each glass. Then I would chatter to pretend guests and throw my head back and laugh and chatter some more. Such things never took place in our home, so I have no idea where I learned this; probably from movies, or television. We got our first television when I was about five years old, therefore, when I saw the television for the first time, I told the people on the screen to shut up and get out. Give me a break; I didn't know what it was. Honestly, I thought it was a home invasion, even though the screen was very tiny.

Anyway, as I was saying, not only did I throw champagne parties, but I also wore imaginary cocktail dresses. Looking at a Sears catalogue, I would find a beautiful cocktail dress and beautiful matching shoes and jewelry, and then I would pretend I was wearing that lovely ensemble. After a while, I began to choose an outfit daily from catalogues, and believed I was wearing them, often wondering why no one was complimenting me. Now that's an imagination. If only Mom and Dad knew what was going on in my head, think of all the money they could have saved by just handing me a catalogue. Oh, how I loved the shoes and slippers! Come to think of it, I never met a shoe I didn't like.

Between the ages of five and eleven, I lived in a house that had a shed/playhouse connected to the back porch. Many hours were spent there where I would "dream up" plays for the neighboring children and then assign a part for whoever showed up that day. There was a large blue sturdy wooden tabletop with sawed off legs that Mom always used for the Christmas tree platform each year, and this made a wonderful stage. My characters were usually at a very sophisticated party where they would dance, drink, and smoke pretend cigarettes, and sometimes there would be a fight scene, and sometimes there would be a real fight; I was a mean director. Mom would come and check on me now and then. I suspect she listened in on some of my plays, because if there was a part where someone had to pretend to be dead, she absolutely forbade such scenes. Apparently, it was okay to drink and smoke.

Smoking cigarettes is bad for your health—duh. How do you know this at the age of twelve and at a time when such a fact has yet to be proven? Sandra used to get a lot of babysitting jobs in the neighborhood when she was a teen. Sometimes she would allow me to tag along so I could play with her charges. After a while she just wouldn't allow me to go to her jobs with her. I had no idea why she suddenly changed her mind. One day, she was babysitting very close to our house, and I knew this, so Mom gave me permission to go and sit with Sandy. Uh-oh! There she sat in the living room smoking a cigarette; she was seventeen. Now, I knew why I was banned. To this day, I wish Mom had not given that permission. We always find a way to blame Mom, don't we? Naturally, I said, "I'm telling Mom."

Sandra said, "Oh no you're not, because if you do, I'm telling her you smoked too."

"That's a lie," I said. So she lit a cigarette and put it in my mouth and held it there until I puffed. Instantly, I liked it. You don't have to believe me, but it's true. I have a very addictive personality, which I discovered years later. Once I got hooked, all I could think of was that I was going to hell. If Sandy hadn't gotten me hooked, someone else would have.

A thief is what I became after that, stealing cigarettes from Dad when he was sleeping. Let me make this clear, that was all I ever stole. But stealing is stealing. I once stole a pack of cigarettes from people for whom I babysat. One day, I passed Mom in the hallway; she smelled the smoke on me. She said, "Have you been smoking?" Oh yeah, by the way, that's when I became a liar.

"No," I said.

"Liar," she said. I tried to tell Mom that she was smelling coffee on my breath. Mom then proceeded to tell me that if *she ever* caught me with a cigarette, she would cram the lit end down my throat. Mom didn't make idle threats, so I made sure she never caught me. In fact, I didn't smoke around her for years after I was married. My social life consisted of sitting around with my friends or cousins, smoking and drinking coffee.

At the age of thirty-three, I discovered alcohol. It was a slow and insidious takeover. My love affair with alcohol lasted until I was forty. That affair was doomed from the start. For one thing, I was a sipper, not a guzzler, and what I sipped didn't stay put for long. Every morning, whatever I sipped found its way back up again. After a while, that got old, so I got help and got out of that mess. God is good! Now my idea of a wild walk is having a few laughs with a few folks, with a cup of coffee and a snack. Is that asking too much? Just so you know, I refuse to go decaf, so *there!*

- 15 -

A Run for the Border

O, Canada! At times, when you're young and poor and bored, you take your rent money and head for Canada, or some equally stupid idea. Just as we were pulling out in the car, the landlord appeared. We said, "Catch you next week." Which we did. Ron Sr. was on vacation and we needed time out from all the drudgery that comes with poverty.

Elvis Presley had just passed away, and the country was in mourning, especially Sandy and her husband, who were going with us, along with their two children and our three children. That's right, nine people in a 1965 Plymouth Fury. All of us, our luggage, and two tents strapped to the hood of the car, traveling from Pennsylvania to Niagara Falls. Now you know this isn't going to turn out well. You should have seen the looks we got from other travelers. It was hard to tell if we were traveling gypsies or hillbillies. No doubt, we were hillbillies. How excited we were to be going to another country! This made us sophisticates in our minds. Never mind that people were laughing at us, what did they know about how we were now world travelers? We chattered and laughed and sang—for the first twenty five miles.

We'd split the seating this way: Ron Sr. was the driver, Jake, the brother-in-law, was up front, Sandy was up front, and their youngest daughter was up front. In the back seat was Diane, the oldest daughter of Sandy and Jake, Rhonda, Ron Jr., Mark, and myself. Mark sat on my lap. Naturally, we had to stop every thirty minutes, because the children's bladders were not in sync. I swear it was the longest ride of my life! One of the pit stops we made in New York stands out in my mind. There was a line for the bathroom, and four of us females were in the bathroom. When we emerged, a woman with a very distinct New York accent remarked, "I should have known it was a bunch of teenagers." I was thrilled; my first sarcasm from a New Yorker. Now I knew I was on my way to being worldly, and to be called a teenager at the age of twenty nine, wowie, a double bonus.

As we got back in the car and continued our journey, Sandy's youngest daughter, Angie, became increasingly annoying. Angie was about ten at that time, and often very mouthy. Her parents' efforts to allay her misbehavior were not effective. My husband had very little tolerance for this type of behavior from children; heck, he didn't allow it from our children. Speaking of which, the ones in the back were no angels either, but I kept them occupied. I can say it would have been better to place Angie in the back seat and place another child in the front, but Sandy was concerned that she might get hurt in the back seat; unfortunately, she was no safer in the front. Angie became more and more irritated and irritable. There were no meds for hyper children in those days. A hand appeared from the driver's side and made a slight contact with her cheek. Yikes! Truth be told, someone had to do something. It's very difficult to focus on driving when another is yelling in your face. Angie screamed a few expletives and then became quiet the remainder of the trip. So did everyone else. Tensions were high.

Finally, after a very long and stressful car ride, we arrived at Niagara Falls. We found a nice, accommodating campground and pitched tent, in silence. Well, not really silence, for some were throwing gear around and mumbling under their breath. Sandra and Ron Sr. weren't speaking to each other, however, Jake and I seemed to have no problem. I was miffed at my husband, but I understood why he felt the need to take control. Hearing the thunder of the falls from where we were camped caused us all to agree that we would leave and go do the very thing for which we had come. Every bit the majestic and awesome sight that we'd heard so much about, it didn't disappoint. God's power and imagination was very evident as we stood there in awe. Upon our return to our sleeping quarters, all was well. Ron Sr.'s apology was given and accepted. Let the fun begin!

Returning to the falls the next day, we ventured around the area and then left to buy some food supplies at a local grocery store. Boy! We were in for a delightful surprise, something that had never occurred to any of us; what a bonanza! The money exchange rate! Our money was worth considerably more at that time. Yahoo! Loading up on lots of food, off we went to chow down and get ready for the evening festivities. Everybody hit the showers in anticipation of going to the local tourist trap that evening. After showering, Rhonda asked, "Mom, where did you put my clothes?" Huh? What clothes? It seemed that Rhonda thought I'd packed her clothes, and I thought that she'd packed her own clothes; after all, she was twelve, and I had to pack for the boys. Clothing was not in the budget; thank God for the exchange rate.

As we left for town that evening, everyone was excited and in a very good mood. When we reached our destination, we all poured out of the car and headed for a fun time. Ripley's Believe It or Not loomed just ahead of us; it could be seen as we walked down the hill from the parking lot. High atop Ripley's building, there was an electric eye with several pupils. Mark was six years old at that time; when he saw that eye, he screamed and headed back for the car. Running after Mark, I broke the strap on my shoe. Getting Mark to settle down and come with us took a lot of convincing, cajoling, and soothing, but eventually, we succeeded. I was the only grown woman walking around town, in and out of the various buildings, in her bare feet. The strap could not be fixed, and there were no shoe retailers to be found. It was kind of like one of those nightmares where you find yourself walking down the street naked. As we sat down to rest on a bench, Mark must have decided that putting a pebble in his nose would keep him calm, it certainly didn't calm his mother. Jake to the rescue! He had plenty of experience at this sort of problem, because Angie used to constantly shove pebbles in her ears when she was younger. With great patience and a steady hand, Jake was able to extract the little booger. A little side note, you seldom see me mention Ron Jr. in our travels, and there's a very good reason for that neglect. You see, when Jr. was traveling and seeing new sights and learning new things, he lived in his own little world. He was completely engrossed in the wonder of it all, and he was absolutely no problem when we were on the road; in fact, the only time we heard from him was when he was hungry. Otherwise, he was a model child; when traveling, that is. Oh, if only we could have lived like traveling gypsies, we'd have saved ourselves a lot of heartache; but that's for another story.

Upon rising the next day, we packed and left and waved goodbye to Niagara Falls. Pouring all nine of us back into the car, we sadly returned to reality.

- 16 -

A Power Trip

Three Mile Island. Got your attention? No, Three Mile Island is not the power trip; rather, it's a small part of this chapter. We lived sixty miles from Harrisburg, Pennsylvania, born and raised there. Let me explain that these are the years before Ron Sr. joined the navy.

In March of 1979, Three Mile Island had a nuclear "accident" that scared the hell out of us all. Even though we lived sixty miles away, who knew how far this stuff could travel? Who knew how serious it was? For a few days, even the experts didn't know, and, to this day, have we been told everything?

In May of 1979, we decided to take a trip to one of the most powerful places on earth— Washington D.C. You would have laughed at us as we reached Harrisburg. We raised up the windows and kept our hands tightly over our mouths and took shallow breaths, as if—well, we were a bit ignorant as to how things worked, and I still am.

D.C. was wonderful! All of the sights were free, and we planned to see all that we could for as long as we could, which was only for a few days. By now, we'd moved up in the world. No using the rent money; this time it was a credit card. Museums, monuments, government buildings; a plethora of entertainment and education.

We love critters of all kinds, so of course, we wanted to visit the zoo. Around and around and around we went, to no avail. There's this big circle of traffic in D.C., and once you get in that circle, you'd better know how to get out; we didn't know squat. Confused and frustrated, my darling husband tried and tried to get us on the right path to the zoo. People were blowing their horns and shaking their fists at us; oh, such rubes we were. Finally, Ron Sr. found a way out after about an hour, and our hero got us to our destination. Rhonda got to see the panda bears that she loved so much, and, the boys got to visit the snake house, which Mom did not love so much. At the end of our critter tour, all that was left to do was "circle" back; I said a little prayer under my breath, and around and around and around we went, with horns blaring and fist shaking once again.

After that fiasco, we decided to go to lunch. We went to the JFK center, where they had a reasonably priced cafeteria. Ron was still a bit shaken up from the traffic ordeal, and after choosing some delicious food from the cafeteria line-up, we all went to find a table. Poor Ron. He dropped his tray of much-needed food. Our plan was to skimp on lunch so we could eat in one of the fancy D.C. restaurants for dinner that evening. A family sharing is a lovely thing, but under these circumstances, it was very sweet. Each of us volunteered something from our trays so that poor Dad wouldn't go hungry. People watching our behavior shook their heads in disgust. No one can say that we didn't leave an impression wherever we went; it just wasn't a good one. Depending on how you looked at it, surely someone must have seen the love and humor in our situation. I really must say that in this day and age, I truly believe people would have been more understanding and kind compared to that time.

After fueling up our bodies as best we could, it was off to the amazing Smithsonian, and then the breathtaking Botanical Gardens. Exhausting and exhilarating, but worth every sore foot, we took in all that we could, because the next day was the big one. The White House!

Since we'd gotten through the remaining day without a hitch, you must know by now that the fancy restaurant that evening would be hilarious. Very swanky. Lovely white tablecloths, lighted candles encased in a small globe for a centerpiece, large sturdy padded chairs and low lighting for ambiance. The waiters were dressed in black pants and white shirts with black ties. Scrumptious aromas emanated from the kitchen. We were seated by a waiter, and after giving our dinner orders, we waited; anxiously, I might add. Soon, the waiter brought a few condiments and water, bread, and rolls and butter to our table. Mark reached across the table to take what he thought was a plate of cheese. I watched him in astonishment as he took a handful of butter. What a mess! Soon, our food arrived. Ron Sr. had ordered a steak with his meal, and, if I may say so, it was a well-deserved steak. Shortly after receiving our meal, Ron announced that the steak was the best he'd ever tasted. I tried to not let that bother me; just let him enjoy. Soon, I began to smell something funky. Sniffing around the table, I concluded that the odor was coming from Ron Sr.'s wonderful steak. I lifted his plate and took a big whiff. Definitely spoiled! Of course, the restaurant was apologetic and replaced his steak with a good one. If this spoiled steak was the best steak he'd ever tasted, what did that say about my cooking? Well, I comforted myself with the thought that he was very tired and hungry.

Our beautiful White House awaited our arrival the next day, along with many other visitors. Absolutely awesome! Of course, there were limited rooms that were open to the public. Carter was president at that time. We actually saw his motorcade drive by the following day. Everything went very smoothly during the tour, and, Rhonda didn't forget to pack for this trip. In fact, Rhonda had chosen a special dress for the White House tour, as I remember. It was a gray sleeveless with a red overlay, and was a perfect fit. She was fourteen at the time, tall and svelte, with long, dark, luscious, thick hair, and big brown eyes. It was quite easy to mistake her for eighteen or perhaps twenty. Some Secret Service men certainly noticed her; in fact, one of them remarked about her pretty dress. Rhonda put her nose in the air and ignored him. Being a mother, I told her she was rude, and could have at least acknowledged him. In retrospect, what was I thinking?

We were completely enthralled with the workings of our nation's capital. It exuded history, beauty, power and a kind of contagious energy. None of us ever wanted to leave. How could we know that less than twenty years later, we would reside in its suburbs, and that my husband would be employed by the Secret Service, and he would survive 9/11?

- 17 -

Driving Miss Judy

Face your fears! You won't know until you try! Give it your all! That's the American way of life, and it's all good advice. In this country, people tend to look down their noses at failure. It's an unacceptable way of life. They see a big L written on your forehead if you don't fit in with the norm. Independence is something for which we strive daily. With my head hung low, I must tell you that I'm not completely independent, and there's a big L written on my forehead.

I faced my fear, I tried, and I gave it my all. But I cannot drive. Believe me when I tell you, I cannot drive. As far as I can see, neither can many other people; they just don't know it. In fact, it seems like many people can't even drive a shopping cart.

Mechanically, I am a big fat zero. Somehow, I'm led to believe that it has something to do with being born left-handed. Back in the day, in some parts of the country, left-handed children were forced by the school to learn to write with their right hand and lead with their right foot. During my first trip to the eye doctor, he noted that my left eye was dominant, so therefore he asked if I was left-handed. Then a light bulb went off in my head! Maybe this was why my sense of direction was so poor. The doc confirmed this possibility, and said,

"Just memorize to go back the same way you went, and you'll be fine." By the way, I'm not bi-dexterous. Okay, now onto the good stuff.

It wasn't unusual for a woman to not drive a car back in the fifties and sixties, at least not where I lived. The town wasn't so big that you couldn't hoof-it wherever you wanted to go. Mom didn't drive; Grandma did, though. That woman was a demon behind the wheel! She never had an accident that I know of; maybe because she was notorious. The other motorists just stayed out of her way. Anyway, when I was in my thirties, I decided to take driving lessons. I want you to know that the whole idea terrified me, but regardless, I wanted to try.

Finding the best driving school in Charleston, South Carolina, where we resided at that time, off I went to seek my independence; after receiving a permit, naturally. My driving instructor was a very lovely and patient young woman. She took me out for many lessons. One day, she invited me to her home for coffee and cake, I guess to soften the blow. She then proceeded to inform me that I simply could not drive. She went so far as to explain that we're not born knowing how to drive, and that there are some folks who just never will. She said that it didn't mean I was stupid, that in fact it's not strange for intelligent people to not drive a car. So, the following week, I got my driver's license. Yep, that's what I just said. She was right, it had nothing to do with being stupid; it had to do with being odd. First time I took my test, I passed it. I told the officer that since he gave me a license, he'd give one to anybody; he threatened to take it back. I assured him that I was just kidding. (I wasn't.)

Nervous Nellie! Oh, most definitely! Soon after becoming a legal driver, my dear friend Gail did all she could to encourage me. I mean, after all, Gail used to ride with the Hell's Angels, and she had no fear, so she was willing to hop in the car and go anywhere with me. One day, she said we should take Mark fishing. Mark loved to fish. So did Ron Jr. We loaded up the car with lunch and fishing gear and Mark, and a very nervous driver, and off we went to the nearest fishing hole. As we were riding through the lane that approaches the water, Gail yelled, "Look at the boat." I slammed on the brakes and nearly gave us all whiplash.

"Where? Where is the boat?" I asked.

Gail said, **"Are you insane? It's in the water.** Where did you think it was?" Then she told me she would be driving us home.

A therapist might be able to help me, I thought, I'll bet you were thinking the same thing. Therefore, I went to get my head shrunk. The shrink deduced that I was afraid of harming others, and that that might be the reason I get so nervous. Well, *yeah*. Hello! This I already knew; at least I knew it was part of the problem. A vehicle is a deadly weapon, after all, and if you place it in the hands of someone who doesn't know up from down, it's only a matter of time. He made a very good suggestion; he said I should start out driving just to the corner and back until I felt comfortable enough to go farther. The problem was that we lived in a cul-de-sac that wasn't a circle, so I had to make a left from the driveway down or up to the corner, and straight out to the road, or else, make a three-point-turn and go back. I decided to make a right and drive to the convenience store a few blocks away. As I was pulling into the parking lot, I didn't want to turn too slowly, because the traffic behind me was honking at my slow speed as it was, so I stayed on the gas pedal, and came inches from slamming into the store. I inched my way back out into the traffic and inched my way home. So much for that idea. My husband tried to help me, He took me to an almost-empty parking lot, and I nearly hit the only parked car in the lot. I agree with you, it's some sort of mental block.

Next, my husband informed me that he was being transferred to Virginia Beach, and he proceeded to say that I, yes, I, would be driving the car there, because he would be driving the moving van. "Are you crazy?" I asked. He then explained that all I had to do is follow the van. "Why?" I screamed. "The navy takes care of the moving, so why am I driving across states when I can't safely drive two blocks?" Ron explained that we'd come out with a big fat check if we did it DIY, and that we needed that check. Being a good navy wife, I agreed to "suck it up," as they say, and endangered my life, my daughter's life, and the lives of many others. Moving day arrived. Ron, Mark, and the dog were in the van, and Rhonda and I were in the car. Ron Jr. was not living with us at that time. We had walkie-talkies so I could scream at Ron every ten miles. And scream I did! One thing that Ron didn't take in to account was that if I stayed directly behind the van, I couldn't see down, or was it up, the road. We stopped for a break and Mark told me that I was weaving all over the road like a drunk. "Because I can't see around the van!" I said.

"You don't need to see around the van; just trust me." said Ron. Ha!

We got separated at a traffic light. I was in the middle of city traffic and panic seared through me. Having absolutely no idea where I was or where to go, I had to rely on the walkie-talkie, but only garbled noises came back to me. I found a place to pull over, and finally, with Mark's help, Ron found us. At that time, we were in North Carolina, and I insisted that we stay there overnight; I was frazzled. The following morning, I said a prayer, threw up, and then off we went for Virginia Beach. All of this transpired in December; therefore, dusk came in late afternoon. Following the van into the parking lot, I pulled up to a cement marker and scrapped it. That did it! I had enough and I told him so. I said, "Get a tow truck or a tow chain, I AM DONE!" He laughed at me. We weren't amused. I was sputtering by this time, and ready to fight. Then I heard the sweetest words ever. "Judy, we're here. Relax!"

As we settled into our new home and life got back to normal— well, as normal as it can when you're part of the greatest military on the planet—once again I wanted to try for my independence. This time, I found myself driving on the interstate with Ron Sr. along to assist me. "Let's practice pulling off and onto the various ramps," Ron said. Okay, because, so far, I wasn't doing too badly; just a little problem with centering the car. So, I drove up the ramp to a convenience store, being careful to not enter the store with the vehicle. We went in the store, got coffee, and came back out. My brain said, "Now, go back the way you came." By this time, it was a way of life to go back the same way I got there. That's right; I went back on the ramp I'd used to get there. Have you ever been on an interstate the wrong way? I emphatically do not suggest that you ever, ever try. My husband screamed, and then commenced to calling me everything but a human. He said it was impossible for anyone to be that stupid unless they were somehow impaired. Can you blame him? I don't. Somehow, under his direction, I was able to get on the roadside, what little there was of it, and back up to the ramp, I got out and he took over. "You're done with driving," he said. I very much agreed. And so I say to you, don't judge me, just thank me. Consider it an ongoing community service.

- 18 -

A Tribute

When the music changes, so does the dance. This, to me, is a very profound and poignant statement. It's a phrase that originates from West Africa, and, of course, is all about music and dance. Personally, I feel that it pretty much sums up life. We sidestep, and we step over, and at times we trot through the things that life throws our way. Oftentimes when we do the two-step forward, we find ourselves doing one step back. Instinctively, we seem to know what direction to move so we can get to the next level. But when life kicks you in the gut and knocks the wind out of you, you're going down to the floor.

On July 3 of 2016, our oldest son, Ron Jr., suddenly and unexpectedly passed away. He was camping in Idaho with a friend and became very ill. The hospital contacted us and told us that he was in liver failure, but there was still a chance that they could help him. Unfortunately, he sneaked out of the hospital in the middle of the night and made his way back to the campground. Two days later, he was rushed to the hospital again; this time there was nothing that could be done. I truly believe it was his wish to die in the great outdoors. He was forty-nine years old.

Jr. had been diagnosed with Multiple Sclerosis about twenty years ago. Thankfully, the only real manifestation of this disease was a slight limp. He wasn't about to allow that to slow him down; even though he also had a blown knee, he just kept going with his insatiable need for adventure. As a child, he consistently ran away from home. His psychiatrist said that the only way to stop him was to break both of his legs, and make sure we broke both of them, because if he had one good leg, he'd still keep going. The man knew what he was talking about. It goes without saying, we didn't break his legs.

Ronnie was a big boy with a big heart. He had a very tough exterior, but he was mush inside. As a youngster, he was always bringing home stray animals, and sometimes, stray people. He couldn't bear the thought of anyone going hungry, so he fed them, from my kitchen.

We hadn't seen Jr. for six years prior to his demise. He'd come to stay with us for two years before that time, which was a wonder in itself. My son and I had always had a strained relationship; I'm of the belief that this was due to the fact that I was always trying to tame him. But I know he loved me. With his bare hands he would have literally killed anyone who tried to hurt me, never realizing that he was the one who hurt me more than anyone.

This tragedy happened while I was birthing the eighth chapter of this book. For weeks, Ron Sr., Mark, and I mourned the loss of our loved one, and, Rhonda, in Wyoming, mourned the loss of her brother. I've never read the death certificate and I never will. A mother is supposed to read her child's birth certificate.

As time went on, I remembered my writings and decided that I wouldn't be able to continue to write my story of humor triumphing over drama. It just all seemed so ironic to me, that there I was, being put to the worse test of my life. Did I still believe all this stuff I was writing?

Suddenly, I thought of my mother and the loss of her first two children and how her sad life went on after the loss of two toddlers in a row. Even so, she was able to giggle and engage in life. Mostly, I thought of Jr. and how very funny he was; his one-liners were original and unmatchable. He could have been a great comedian. Most of all, he wouldn't have wanted me to leave you on this sad note that I felt compelled to share with you. He would have said, "Always" leave them laughing, Mom." Therefore, I decided that I will not be a hypocrite, and so I continued with the writing from chapter eight on to here, so kindly read the epilogue.

Epilogue

From There to Here
No more running through the house.
No more snot wiped on my blouse.
No more keeping up a pace.
No more children in my face.

Does that little ditty sound sad to you? Or perhaps it sounds mean. Neither one is intended. To me, it spells FREEDOM. Since I was twelve years old, I've been looking after somebody's children. First, the neighbor children, then, when my nieces and nephews came along, I gladly helped out while the parents worked. I came home from school and sterilized bottles, made formula, changed diapers, and fed babies. Then I had my own, and no one helped, but at least I had the experience. Of course, after that, I helped with the grandchildren, a lot, for years. Then, there was a great-grand, whom I had quite often. And then there were none. Suddenly, everyone became independent, and, after all, isn't that what we want? The swinging door has been closed for some time now. A big adjustment, for sure, and it wasn't easy. Being the survivor that I am, I suddenly realized that this is a good thing. My life is different, not over. At first I felt like I was sent out to pasture. So what? Pastures are fields with grass and flowers and lots of elbow room, and not to mention, peaceful. A pasture is not a cemetery or a nursing home; it's a place to run free! Not only that, but I no longer have to put up with all the criticism from young parents who like to tell me about all the things I'm doing wrong. And the best part is that when things do go wrong in their happy little lives, THEY CAN'T BLAME ME! As a retired childcare giver, and with Ron now retired, we have lots of free time. Oh no, we don't!

Somehow, some way, we find ourselves busier than we've ever been in our lives. Doing what? I'll be damned if I know. Could be that rigor mortis, I mean arthritis, has slowed us down so much that it takes an hour to do what we used to do in a half hour. Don't let your mind go there, that is not what I mean. Seriously, though, what is going on here? Admittedly, we are late sleepers, and instead of taking an afternoon nap, I just sleep until ten or eleven a.m. unless there's an appointment. We try to not make morning appointments.

There's no real social life to speak of. Mark has remained very loyal and kind to us, so we see him socially on occasion. Sometimes we meet friends for lunch or dinner. All I know is it's definitely not our social life that's keeping us so busy. We don't travel. Speaking for myself, I had enough of that when Ron was in the navy, even though we always managed to stay on the East Coast. We've done a bit of volunteer work in the past, but we have no time for that anymore.

Bella and Braxton run our lives, along with the doctors, that much I do know. Both the dogs and the docs keep us up and running; they just have different agendas. You see, the dogs want us up and running so we can look after them, and the docs want us up and running so we can take care of ourselves.

There is a shopping trip to the grocery store almost every day (which, by the way, is where I do my reading. You know, fat content, calories, expiration dates, carbohydrates, etc.). After squinting through the fine print, I buy what I want. The reason for these frequent excursions is simple; we always forget something we need, and we always need something. Sure, I make a list, and then I forget the list or I omit an item. Whatever At least I get my reading time out of the way.

Downtime is a rare commodity around here. We walk the dogs every day, feed them two times a day, and take them on car rides. Man! They are spoiled. Doing household chores and cooking daily, keeping appointments, whew! Then, there are the neighbor's pets. I go out and give them treats and talk to them. Heck, I know them better than I know the owners. Also, I look after all of my yard creatures, especially watchful for the baby birds in the warm weather.

At first, Christmas seemed a little sad and lonely. Not anymore. Christmas is now as Jesus intended it to be: peaceful, calm and enjoyable. You see, I no longer feel compelled to go shopping for worthless junk to give to ungrateful family members. Nor do we scramble to drag the tree and decorations down from the attic to impress people who only show up on Christmas Eve long enough to exchange gifts, eat the food I set out, and then get out of Dodge because they have better places to go to, especially on Christmas Day. Ron Sr., Mark, and I enjoy a very decadent Christmas dinner using the money we would have spent on frivolous presents for frivolous people. God bless us all, everyone.